Visions and Revisions

Murray Bodo, OFM

Visions and Revisions

© 2009 Murray Bodo, OFM

Book and Cover Design: Veronica A. Martinez
Cover Image © Paolo Grimaldi
Image of Fr. Murray Bodo on back cover taken by Fr. Jack Wintz, OFM

No part of this publication may be reproduced, stored in a retrieval system or transmitted in any form or by any means, electronic, mechanical, photocopying, recording, or otherwise, without written permission of the publisher.

For information regarding permission, write to Tau publishing, Attention: Permissions Dept, 1422 East Edgemont Avenue, Phoenix, AZ 85006

ISBN-10:1-935257-09-9
ISBN-13: 978-1-935257-09-7

First Edition: May 2009
10 9 8 7 6 5 4 3 2 1

For re-orders and other inspirational books and materials visit our website at Tau-publishing.com

Published and Printed in the USA by:

Tau-publishing.com
Words and Works of Inspiration

And time for a hundred indecisions
And a hundred visions and revisions
Before the taking of a toast and tea.

T.S. Eliot, "The Love Song of J. Aflred Prufrock"

In the 800th Year of the Founding of
the Franciscan Way of Life: 1209-2009

Contents

I

Writer's Block	7
Dry Sonnet	8
Wounded Sonnets, Songs of Praise: A Corona	9
Clare di Favarone and the Moon	12
Saint Francis and the Fish	13
Saint Francis at Collestrada	14
Saint Francis at Greccio	15
Stigmata	16
death at the porziuncola	17
At Saint Clare's Mirror	18
Benozzo Gozzoli at Monte Falco	19
Mass for the Feast of Saint Francis	20

II

Grace	29
Soul-making	32
Genesis and Morning Lauds	33
Silence	34
Pilgrim's Hymn	35
Praying	36
After Wind and Rain	37
Night and the Well	38
Ash Wednesday	39
Dark Angel	40
Georges Rouault's, "Vieux Faubourg" 1917-1927	41
Island Chapel	44
Paradox	45

III

Memoir	49
Starlight and Candlelight	50

Ramage	51
Cousins	52
English Lesson	53
Visitant	54
Enemy	55
Mining Camp Photo, 1920's	56
Anniversary	57
At a Certain Age	58
Hearing Things	59
Someone's World	60
Even the Birds of the Air	61
For Denise Levertov	62

IV

water, wind, and waves	65
Fog and Clearing	66
Emma	67
On the Train Outside Lewes	68
Wives of Bath	69
Aldeburgh Beach	70
Shelley	72
Believing	73
Pilgrimage	74
Diary	76
crossing the divide	77
Return	78
Painting Above My Desk	79
On the Road East	80
Home	81
Tree Sentencing	82
Apocalyptic Deer	83
Bells	84
Revision	85
Afterword	87
Notes	89

I

Writer's Block

> When I lose my center
> of gravity
> I can't fly:
> – Denise Levertov

He wants to write the hills of Umbria,
swallows frantic for flying insects
that shoot like hot cinders from chimneys.

He wants to feel the heat penetrate each
stone upon stone till Assisi houses
pile into ovens pink with baking noons.

But having lost his center, no one
to catch his fall, his words refuse to fly
like the lark St. Francis became.

He tries to write the airplane taking off
but hears, instead of peaceful fountains,
flak and turbulence pounding in his ears.

The computer screen lights up his words.
Engines burn smooth; the lines try to lift
but rattle and fall just before take off.

He tries again, despite the turbulence.
Not wanting to, he fastens his belt, leans
forward and types, "I cannot fly alone."

Dry Sonnet

So. It's a gray day, the rain
sizzling on the hot veranda.

I remember other rain
cool and clean on Assisi streets.

Here it is humid, even
after the slant of rain blows through

like regret without forgiveness,
separation without truth.

A warm wind's drying the rain,
waves of oppressive heat rising.

I remember dry sirocco
and no rain on Subasio

like forgiveness without the
rain of reconciliation.

Wounded Sonnets, Songs of Praise
A Corona for Margaret Carney, OSF

How to praise God with great humility
has something to do with his father's mouth
open in disbelief in the bishop's
cortile as Francis lays his clothes at
his father's feet and walks away from his
mother standing behind his father   eyes
red with grief and knowing that he will not
return from his mad walk toward what she fears
is a phantasm of his sick brain which
walking can't find a cure for although
Francis finds it almost immediately
when robbers throw him in a ditch and laugh
at the nakedness beneath his threadbare
sackcloth tunic and he is unashamed.

Sackcloth tunic and he is unashamed
reminds him now of Lady Poverty
how naked she embraced the naked
Christ homeless where she alone lay upon
the cross with him, his disciples fleeing
that intimacy for something less than
union which only stripping consummates
like now as Francis sets aside former
banquets for this gathering of scraps that
fall from tables overfull of food not
eaten by those who say they know the bread
life-giving and eternal   yet drop it
on Assisi streets as they make their way to
church that eats a bread white and unleavened.

continued...

Church that eats a bread white and unleavened
and no other   eats Christ the Lord without
the crust hard, its mold scraped off discarded,
a Christ who does not exist for he is
one bread one body, whole only when poor
ones are one and one is many who need
someone to bring them back to the giver
of bread to make of them new seeds that die
into wheat backlit in Umbrian light
brightly honed to Christ's sharp stigmata
that cuts through body and into the soul,
a two-edged light that separates and brings
together body and soul, sheaf and sheaves
body soul bread wheat, human and divine.

Body soul bread wheat, human and divine.
As they are to one another, so is
Francis walking toward what the walk becomes,
pilgrimage as a way of prayer, of church.
As he says to Pope Innocent, "A poor
woman lived in the desert. The king passed
by her hovel and seeing her he loved
her and had sons by her too many to feed.
The king himself fed and clothed them.
Lord Pope, Jesus Christ is the king and I
am the poor woman." And the Pope agrees.
Francis becomes mother to his brothers,
the Poor Lady Clare and her sisters and
all born of Francis and Christ on the road.

continued...

All born of Francis and Christ on the road
take to the road outside Assisi's walls
like Clare their first daughter who takes their words
Gospel and rule, weaves her own patterned life:
poor ladies of the King's wayside castle.
Knights errant, the brothers vie for Lady
Clare's hand, poor daughter of the Lord and his
desert bride who go before them always,
portable courts of church-making among
those fallen by the wayside, the birds and
animals, plants and heavenly bodies
brother sun and sister moon and all things
through and with and for and in which we learn
how to praise God with grand humility.

Clare di Favarone and the Moon

Full moon over
Mount Subasio
high above
father's tower.

I love the moon
a burning
mirror of light
invisible.

Or when it's
crescent, a wry
smile before
it disappears.

Someday when
the moon's
a waning sliver
of smile,

I'll slide down
into the vale
dark and close
with mystery.

Saint Francis and the Fish

Fish won't jump
 as water won't boil
  stared at.

It happens out of
 the corner of
  the eye

when we're looking
 elsewhere –
  the way

Saint Francis looked
 at waves roiled
  by wind

and something stirred
 within, and he
  looked again

and saw fish
 jumping and listening
  to him

who was no longer
 staring at
  the same waves.

Saint Francis at Collestrada

    The new shopping mall
            on the way to Collestrada
turned our attention.
            He fell near here, armor torn off,
prisoner of war.

    But now we shop for
            computer cases to protect
our armor, the words
            that shop his life for quick stories
of his slow making

    in a Perugian dungeon.
            He sold no cloth there,
he wove the ragged strands of soul,
            he stored other goods.

We drive instead to Perugia
            and roam the open
market for buyable antiques.
            Nothing valuable's

for sale in that blinding noonlight.
            Numb, we find trifles,
we look for a trattoria,
            check our purchases.

We agree it's been a good day;
            mall and market made
for an easy Sunday foray.

Saint Francis at Greccio, 1223

Mists lift from morning fields
below Greccio. He yields

again to dawn's mystery
that feels like a victory.

The dark is yesterday, night
behind and before what might

become eternal morning,
no more fear or warning

of everlasting dark, the day
an endless, lightsome way

that moves movelessly with Him,
the eternal Babe within.

Stigmata

    Surrender
        as to that burning bird
           half wings

half a sort of man,
    burns Francis
        inside out.

He lifts
    drawn upward
        by wings

beating, and one
    like a man
        still as love's core

the trembling feathers
    holding the man
        steady

the wounds
    opening to Francis
        wound to wound

settting him aflame
    as when
        a baby's

startled
    into the light
        by pain.

death at the porziuncola

francis of assisi, 1182-1226)

      vision of the valley at sunset:
      russet to blood red

      you lived there oozing red
      at the end a kind of sunset

      your bed the earth red
      your wounds a sunset

      the larks a flash of red
      into the blazing sunset

At Saint Clare's Mirror

I look into the mirror
there is no face

I look into the mirror
of no place

I am the mirror
I wait for you

to look into the mirror
of who

you will be
when you are mirror

waiting to see
through another's eyes

looking into the mirror
of your eyes

Benozzo Gozzoli at Monte Falco

Heat scalds the hills, the ginestra
droops and sways in soggy wind.

Inside the church – become museum –
Saint Francis, cool and bright,

lives his life as Gozzoli saw
whose painting brings outside into

frames and inside into color and
prayer into gesture: that hand blessing,

lifting outside and inside lightly upward
away from this profitable church museum

where Gozzoli's purveyors hide the Poverello
from those the artist lifts beyond the frames of art.

Mass for the Feast of St. Francis of Assisi

In Honor of the 800th Anniversary of His Way of Life, 1209-2009

Introit

In fall ginestra
on Mount Subasio
fades, and poppies
on the plain below
are gone till seeds
rise where they fell

Kyrie

For the homeless man
who sleeps on the steps
of the building we pass
on our way to concerts,
Kyrie Eleison

For us who pass by
the homeless woman
who sleeps on the steps
of the building we pass
on our way to ball games,
Christe Eleison

For rich nations
who let the homeless
sleep soundly on steps
of the buildings they pass
on the way to war,
Kyrie Eleison

continued...

Gloria

Here is robin
digging for worms.
Praised be you, O Lord.

Here is worm
fattening on soil.
Praised be you, O Lord.

Here is fox
who reddens lamb hill.
Praised be you, O Lord.

Here is sun
warming the earth
that fattens the worm.
Praised be to you, O Lord.

Here is moon
that lights the way
of lamb hill fox.
Praised be you, O Lord.

Here is lark,
angel who sings
Glory to God in the highest.
Praised be you, O Lord.

Here is the highest, Lord God,
Almighty Father.
Praised be you, O Lord.

continued...

Here is Most High
made most low, a worm
in the hands of enemies,
Jesus Christ, only Son
who descends to worm
to fox and robin and us.
Praised be you, O Lord.

Here is Jesus Christ, God
and Man, Peace of His
People on earth.
Praised be you, O Lord.

Here is the Holy One,
Jesus Christ, the Most High.
Praised be you, O Lord.

Here is Jesus Christ
with the Holy Spirit
breath of the Father.
Praised be you, O Lord.

Here is the Father,
Creator of all.
Here is the Son,
Who takes away sin,
gives us His Spirit.
Praised be you, O Lord.

Here is Trinity in Unity.
Be our Mercy
receive our prayer.

Praised be you, O Lord,
through worm and fox
robin lamb and us.

continued...

Praised be you, O Lord,
Hill and Altar. Amen.
Praise to you, O Lord
tree branches burning. Amen.
Praise to you, O Lord,
Risen Lamb, Heavenly Food. Amen.

Credo

We believe in God
who falls in night
from Mary's womb onto
the manger's cold floor

We believe in God
who sends God
who falls in night
from Mary's womb onto
the manger's cold floor

We believe in the Spirit
sent by God who rose
from the tomb of God
who fell in the night
from Mary's womb onto
the manger's cold floor

We believe in God
who lives in those
who believe in God
who fell and rose and sent
the Spirit to all who believe
in God who fell from
the cross into Mary's arms
from whose womb he fell
in night into the cold
dark tomb
continued...

We believe in God
of bread and wine that becomes
God who fell in night
from Mary's womb onto
the manger's cold floor
that became his tomb

We believe in God who
forgives the sins of those
who believe in God who
fell in night from Mary's
womb into the cold earth's
tomb

We believe in God
who rose from death's
tomb taking with him
those who believe
in the God who fell
in night from Mary's
womb into the cold tomb

We believe in God
whose Church is all
who believe in God
who fell in night
from Mary's womb onto
death's bright floor

Homily

The greatest evil is the refusal of repentance, to deny the truth of your sins and thereby to create your own truth.

continued...

And if you are powerful enough, your own
truth becomes the truth and therefore
no one is guilty.

What would have been repentance
becomes the transference of evil onto
those whose actions remind you of

what you deny in yourself
to prevent guilt and repentance
and God's forgiveness.

Sanctus

Kadosh, Sanctus, Holy
Breaker of Bread, God of all.
Heaven and earth are your glory.
Hosanna inside us
and in the highest.

Blessed is He whose
Name is the Highest.
Hosanna to the Highest
inside us.

Agnus Dei

You, God, are Lamb
led willingly to slaughter
silent not bleating.
Miserere nobis.

You, God, lie on the altar
a sacrifice for us
silent singing.
Miserere nobis.

continued...

You, God, submit to fire
that burns our sins.
Bleating Spirit
Dona nobis pacem.

Meditation After Communion

Like this
the laying down of life
Like this
diminishment
Like this
the lying down in death
Like this laying down
the surrender
Like surrender
this laying down of life
Like this
the surrender
the laying down
the lying down
Like this
the increase
that is diminishment
Like this
the loving
Like this
is God
Like
us

Grace

As on a still-river summer
afternoon, only violent
boats knifing the placid surface,

you wait for the unexpected
and windless waves start to stir,
an almost unnoticed roll you

knew was there beneath your seeing,
a flow moving deep toward what you
cannot see, but choose to believe.

continued...

2.

It's not just waiting
      something must be given,
an attention, perhaps, or
          surrender
as when, not watching
         the bobber,
you miss something
         tugging
pulling the float
         under
however briefly
         and when
you look
      all is as it was
like taking oneself
         to prayer
and being
         elsewhere
not seeing what
         is stirred
not hearing
         the heard

continued...

3.

As if it were easy
your own waters turbulent

your boat capsizing
and even learned prayers

memorized, dumb at the lips.
You scan the horizon

to keep from vertigo and see
across the troubled waves

Christ steady on the horizon
his cross your equilibrium.

soul-making

      the way sycamores shed
              their bark, say,
     or petals fall from tulips
            pistil naked

     it is renewed, the earth
            and the human
     spirit: that shedding, that
            naked cry
     and mulching and decay
              of what must die

     delay though we try

            spirit then
     within and after what's
              naked and can die

Genesis and Morning Lauds

1.

That said, He left off saying
Until the Spirit playing
With the Father, sent the Son

Word and done then become one
All saying now the actions
Of Jesus, his transactions.

2.

Praise, like waking, rises slow
Mornings when sleep falls slower
And memory fails origins.

That said, we leave off praising
Until grace, the Spirit's gift,
Praises when we sing as one.

Silence

Could God be silence, after all
After all the words, rituals
Proclamations, incantations?

After the hymns and processions
After tears and lamentations,
Could silence be the answer?

Silence loud with divinity
No words, no thoughts, no images
Could silence be the God of prayer?

As when, silent, he wrote in sand
And she – smelling his feet – heard?

Pilgrim's Hymn

He is the icon on the wall,
voice of silence, no voice at all.

In sleepless night, he is steady breath,
breathing us to the life of death.

He walks ahead, cracked feet bleeding,
broken heart, but interceding.

He crosses borders on the road,
he carries others' greedy load.

He gathers garbage, cuts our lawn,
works as hard when we've moved on.

He disappears, then reappears
when we have nothing left but tears.

He is our last horizon,
mystery we fix our eyes on:

Praying

As when a southerly breezed brushes wavelets
against the shore, and you wait
and let the breeze cool your legs –

or when gulls glide, their cries muted
and everyone's playing too far away to be heard
and you are doing nothing –

not even seeing or listening or glancing
at your watch or at
the gestures of swimmers –

and you are no one anyone sees
and you don't even know you're breathing
and no one calls you –

and only afterwards
you see you were burning
in the sun.

After Wind and Rain

    Pain within and
        and all around you
            when suddenly
    everything's awash with rain

    a cloudburst
           swift, short,
    and you smell the rain,

    the pain forgotten
        like childbirth afterwards
    or depression
           lifted.

More rain,
        another interval
of something dropping earthward,

    the pain is now muscles
              relaxing
    like the hands, say,
        after reefing the sail
    in a storm –

    or taut nerves
             letting go
    as you watch hawks glide – though

    the hawks are taut
        as they glide effortlessly
    for you –

    or the way bent palm trees
        straighten and sigh
    when the winds die.

Night and the Well

Pigeons sleep on railings of
no windows opposite mine.

Vacant black sky interrupts
the dry well's stones where I lie.

Hopeful laughter echoes from
the street above, where last night

I thought I heard an old voice
promise, Here is a way out.

Today someone's slow footsteps
pad away from my hearing.

Now are the fragments of light
impossible constellations.

Ash Wednesday

Crossed with ashes, I walk the beach
where out at sea dark clouds threaten
lukewarm sand of plovers and gulls.

Three bundled matrons play cards like
terns phalanxed against darkening
waves. They hunker down determined.

A lone banded pelican stops
and watches me look at him look
at me. He stands there, a ragged

symbol of this day's signature.
He does not move except to stretch.
A strong cold wind ruffles the soft

feathers of his golden crown, his
sword-like bill bodes the Friday when
he pierces his side to feed us.

He follows me when I walk, he
stops when I stop. He lets me watch.
At last he flies away alone

zig-zagging the shoreline into
a blur of amplitude toward
the lightening mackerel clouds.

Dark Angel

You appear at midnight
from unimagined depths,

your face wet with blood
the return has cost you.

You come in black night and
not at dawn, a clean song

filling the room where I wake.
You come almost an ogre.

You are silent as the dead
and yet alive about to speak.

Your open mouth breathes out
and I am swallowed up in

a rush of cold air that sucks
me down the corridor

of your escape from the tomb.
You carry me bodily

down and down until we break
into an unremembered place

of one who seems light dark,
dark light unimaginable.

You breathe me out again and
I fall back into time's clocks.

I have no idea where I've been,
I leave the night light on.

Georges Rouault's "Vieux Faubourg" 1917-1927

"Sunt Lachrymae Rerum" – Georges Rouault

war's brown stain's
now a huge tree
its blackened branches
perched with blue
gouache becoming birds

the russet suitcase
of man with animal
face cast down,
his body, swathed
with two white
tablets of the law,
passes a red stain
framing the brown
face of the suffering
Christ, head bowed
for the animal-man's
plight – the blight
of exile from black-
windowed houses

black the borders,
stained the glass,
blue the light

beneath the road
become tree trunk,
it crouches, creature
half child, half man,
half woman, clown

continued...

dwarfed, crushed by
roads and trees whose
stain's relieved by
pastel blue, the shirt
of man embracing
woman in a corner
of war's brown-
black smudge
over which blue
impasto tries to
embrace the couple
the houses, the road

from a cruciform blue
wash a face emerges
crucified, a stained
glass window into
2 Corinthians 1:4-5:
He comforts us in all
our afflictions and thus
enables us to comfort
those in trouble, with
the same consolation
we received from him –
says the gallery label
blue's trying

continued...

to form alpha
and omega,
the frame's
the same blue
trying to seep
through black
borders where
blue light's
beginning to
hide the stains
of the crushed
photogravure
city

from afar,
as stain glass
windows are,
it's clear that
all the blue
is only sky
trying to
break through

Island Chapel

As after rain, the sun flooding
the painting above the altar

of Simeon holding at last
the Savior in his ancient arms,

the dark outlines of statues gone
like the clouds that drove us indoors –

As when our clothes began to dry
and peel from our legs in the warmth

of the light-filled room, the candles
cozy as small electric fires,

so is your return, absent one,
after the frigid years of months

when, like the sun, you hid behind
something like clouds impenetrable

to a heart cold, dark as this church
before sun lit the walls like fire.

Paradox

1.

They say time
      is eternity,
death
      is life:

that paradox:
      what seems
is not what is.

The hard,
      in the doing,
is easier than
      what seemed
the better choice.

Like penance
      when it's
love,
      a kind of
solidarity
      with humanity.

2.

Or climbing
      when it's
the way to
      the summit
and not
      the summit

reached
      the hard way
when the tired
      muscles let go

& "here" is
      no longer time
but arrival you
always have.

Or the light
      on pained,
darkened faces
      just before
they die
      as if
they now hold
      what they
behold.

III

Memoir

As when, looking at the clouds,
you know they'll not be there again –
   not that way, anyway.

And what you're feeling can't be marked
   by clouds
but only by your looking at them –

as when you remember looking out
   the window at clouds –
their changing shapes – and something
has changed in you that you wanted to tag
   to them.

Instead there's only you changed
trying to remember
looking at the clouds

and what it felt like before you realized
it couldn't be marked or tagged
or remembered.

Starlight and Candlelight

Like the stars in a quadrant
         not the sky – but
the mind, say, or the soul –

the saints shine
and I stare
and remember
how they shone when
I was a boy.

But like the stars
I seldom see them now,
except
         on nights
like this one
as I sit on the porch
with the stars
above the palms

              the crickets
scraping,
              my pen
scratching
         across the candlelit page.

Ramage

Memories crowd my desk where photographs
Cloud the space where I write to clear a way.
Though decades divide their shroud of poses
From the skewed contingencies I've bowed to
– that claimed looking back is not allowed –
I'm now not cowed by those strict minds who
co-opted the vowed life, kept me from those
faces that here beckon, silent and proud.

Cousins

You're 2 and I'm 3.
We hold the reins of

the once-upon horse
that shivers.

Before-death years remember
what the in-between years

erased: faces
that now remember

we were there,
legs too short for stirrups

hands tiny on the pommel
eyes on whoever took the trouble

to lean on the old De Soto
and take our photo.

English Lesson

"Poor Charlie Chaplin,
him got no febbra,
him got no shoes on,
poor Charlie Chaplin…"

"Febbra" is sweater when he
at four, made the melody.
"Always singing," they said,
those Italians now dead

who thought that "febbra"
must be the frayed sweater
they'd worn across the ocean –
a new word in a new nation.

Visitant

You came first in my
play chalice of water
that I changed to red
wine by dropping candy
into it, stirring well
for consecration.

You came later
in wine less sweet
before the miracle
happened: your
return, the wine
stirring, sweetening

And all the years
between, and all
the years between:
what seemed like
mere routine.

Enemy

Like hearing a melody
that triggers something done
which once we were afraid
to remember, meeting you
was only fearful anticipation.
I celebrate this late summer
and wish that long before
I could have made my peace
with memory. But, you see,
what you did was so present,
dear enemy, that I failed
to trust I'd moved on. Like
the pheasant flown from
the echoing corn, I was still
afraid of that dangerous
field of dogs and hunters.

Mining Camp Photo, 1920's

They look fiercely forlorn
these three children,
my mother and
her two brothers.
Something's fled
from their eyes,
the little girl
her clenched fist
clutching a flower
like a secret,
the little boy
aiming his flower
like a gun
as he stands
in the borrowed army coat
daring anyone anything.
They hold the hand
of their little brother
like the adults
they've had to become,
the youngest between them,
fending off
for as long as it takes,
clutching hand and flower
as if they knew
this is what would be.

Anniversary

The way on this April day
the frost crusts my Ford Taurus
is the feel of remembrance:

your grave heaped with frozen dirt,
elk droppings like crystal marbles
strewn in a panic of flight.

Thaw, I pray, cruel April.
Then, as if mercifully,
more than weather relents,

and you are there, feet stomping
and together we're praying
at your heaped earth, both of us

older, I seven decades
like the you we're staring at
shuffling our feet for some warmth.

At a Certain Age

there will be an
incompleteness,
something missed, gone

though he goes on
tries not to know
or remember.

This is where he's
arrived, not what
he had desired –

a last nightfall
or, with luck, first
light of morning.

Hearing Things

Always they sing here,
their melodies, their harmonies

sounding from a glance
in the mirror say, the way

I hear things as they
did, or the color of my voice,

or a musical choice
that was theirs and I'd forgotten.

They sing here now in
couplets that reach for more than rhyme,

that want to hold on
lest they vanish like their voices,

the loved ones. How can
song be anything other than

notations to one's
desire that they, so loved, shall live.

Someone's World

– looking at Andrew Wyeth's sketches for "Christina's World"

Now it's woods that used to be
thoughts and feelings I walked in
and out of when you were ill –

the way the field below Olson
House was Christina's way out
of what confined her spirit

and now's a field empty of
all that yearning and struggle
except for Wyeth's painting –

like a poem that tries to feel
what it was like to walk in
the woods and not know if you

would make it or lie down
instead with those before you
as when I would walk your dog

alone and feel Christina's
pain when Alvaro died
and she saw the field far as

eternity where she would lie
a month later. The hurt then, as
now, is more than paint or words.

Even the Birds of the Air

As if they knew, the gulls
this morning between lulls
of the crashing waves, lifted
beaks where sand had shifted.

Something was missing they
didn't see: your coy way
of slipping crumbs between
scattered shells. Was their keen

for something more than food –
a hand, a voice, a mood –
they understood was your
way of stirring water-

birds to breakfast and song,
your care sweet and gone?

For Denise Levertov

A line that didn't work:
there were so many then
when I'd have you open
<u>Poet in the World</u>, perk
my line-breaks to sharpen,
show why breath broken
makes the difference to
word-songs spoken.

Now that you are elsewhere,
I listen to your notes, their
scales and line-breaks; I hum
your breathed rhythm
and hear a shadowed ache
sing and pause and break.

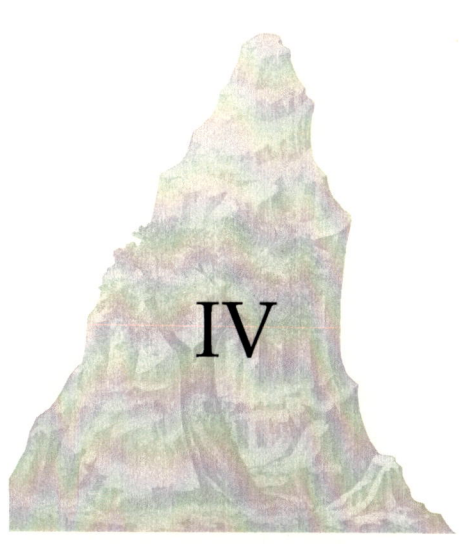

IV

water, wind, waves

we're crossing the ocean

rough water, 7 force winds
18 foot waves

we see nothing
thinking there's nothing to see

but water, wind, waves
no birds, no mountains, no trees

we're crossing the ocean
looking for land, missing

the water, wind, waves
all their plumed display

their crests, their green
trunks and leaves.

we're crossing the ocean

Fog and Clearing

Like a heavy fog close off
the Grand Banks of Newfoundland,
the ship's horn sounding every
three minutes, words befuddle
sight sometimes, though vision may
be clearer for the fog they
navigate toward light subtler
than the sheen the sun reveals.

Words, like fog, can cloud the eye
to look more closely into
the undefined, the obscure
until the congeries of
words transform our common sight
into image and insight.

Emma

I linger, like Henry James,
in Southampton; the ship's wake
shakes my soul. It departs, as
I arrive, in fog and mist.

Is it aging that makes clouds
greyer and the late summer
chill to lift fritters of fear,
uncovering soul's zero?

In <u>The Standing Order</u> pub
I sit next to Jane Austen;
her prim lithograph avoids
my staring. She lived here once.

And once I'd have warmed to know
that layered fact, which now stares
blankly back at her averted
eyes. I've yet to read <u>Emma</u>.

On the Train Outside of Lewes

The man walking his field
with the white dog,
fog on the chalked cliffs.

We speed to Brighton,
Pinkie and Rose
across the aisle from me:

*Detroit, 1957. We're
reading Graham Greene
for English class:*

*Brighton Rock explodes
sheltered clerics' souls.
Evil smokes like fog.*

Pinkie and Rose stare
blankly at fields
empty of man or dog.

They and the fog
stay with the train
all the way to Brighton.

Wives of Bath

In the public gardens of Bath
wives sprawl on the grass unabashed
by the leering young men who sniff
about for experienced sex.

The tales of these languid wives
belong to boys' imaginations,
the wives' usual lives quiescent
as grass and Sundays in the park.

But among them surely there are
some who, like Chaucer's Wife of Bath,
could tell a tale or two to please
a randy boy or curious nun.

Aldeburgh Beach

1.

Solid brown shingles front
the sun-sequined sea.

The end of August – all
is calm, except the air.

It turns to a small wind
freshening with the far cries

of Iraqis, Israelis, Lebanese.
A sailboat

glides past, unaware
of the gale-cries.

The sea is sail perfect,
too vast to reveal

the roiling elsewhere
far from this rippling sea.

continued...

2.

The child watches Dad
fly the kite for her
then turns and picks up
pebbles instead.
Dad, oblivious,
shows off his aerial skill
to the same
bored little girl
he tried to impress
years ago
as he dove from the high cliff
while she wrote in the sand
letters to Billy
the boy who played football,
oblivious of Dad's
desperate acrobatics.

Shelley

Waiting for words he
arrived in Florence
Santa Maria Novella.

The plaque, as you exit
the train station and
cross the street, reads

Here Percy Bysshe Shelley
wrote "Ode to the West Wind"
worked on "Prometheus Unbound."

"Here" is the location; "where"
is no longer there, replaced
by a building whose archway

leads into a windless
inner courtyard where
cars park and unpark.

Believing

Someone said that sycamores
shed their bark all the year long.

I don't look that up because
if it's false, what explains how

they survive Roman traffic,
its olio of poisons?

Don't trees breathe in, too?
I'll not look that up either.

Someone said animals grieve,
their feelings can be hurt like

us who want to believe they
can't. Otherwise we'd have to

stop kicking the dog, notice
the roadside's abandoned ones

and then have to see people
among them as we speed by.

We believe, it seems, what we
decide we have to believe.

Pilgrimage

How you come at last
   to not feeling
      you can return –

not the same journey
   at least –
      The dome of St. Peter's

in Rome through the window
   of the rented room
      as before

now has become
   the stone it is
      and not

the rush of glory
   anticipated
      year after year

continued...

like the thrill of
  "God is love" followed
  by the moment

when promises seem
  mere words and
    deception

and you cannot return
  to the thrill of it
    the stones
being thick with
  "Why have you
    forsaken me?"

feeling then – slowly –
  a turning not
    unlike returning.

Diary

It's the early morning hours
before daylight when rain streaks
the windows as the ship crosses
the Atlantic three days out
from Southampton.

The quiet's rudely broken by
a backnoise of elevator music
omnipresent, it seems, in any
man-made space.

What could have been grace
turns to dismay that even here
mid ocean the screech
of an unwelcome sax
grates in the ear.

crossing the divide

    that tiredness, as after a long trip

    that feeling the road is hurtling
      you out of control
        instead of you driving it

    that wish for home to move
      faster toward you
        or at least as fast as you're
      being hurled toward it

    that need to stop
        and dig deep into any soil

    that nausea of movement
      for movement's sake

    that trembling fear
      you've still not outrun
      what you're running from

    that forward precipitation
      that's like a roller coaster
        gone wild

    that need to look beyond the road
      to the still landscape
        whizzing by

    that horizon as still point
      that steadies

    the disappearing cows
      slow-grazing the pace
        you long for

Return

Once wet words crackle
from memory's stark sand hills,
their song bitter as cactus,
their taste strong as sage.

A snapped twig opens syllables
scorched dry and fierce as sun:
rattlesnake and scorpion,
shack collapsing, its rusted

bucket rattling against the
handle of the cracked pump
it whacks in wind that
sandblasts a steer's carcass.

Old scars and bruises.
Desert air that aches
with what one loses.

The Painting Above My Desk

The Navajo horsemen forever
riding towards me, the red cliffs
pink in the indistinguishable
light blurred between dawn and dusk.
Puffed dust like cigarette memories
smudged behind them, they ride easy
in the saddle, their steady parade
about to overtake me
when the hooves halt at the border between the painting and the paint.

On the Road East

Between midnight and 2 when you
wake to your own coughing into
the silence of a rented room
on Route I-Something toward where you've
pointed your hope of arrival,
night is light as words remembered:
Surely darkness shall hide me and
night shall be my light, for darkness
and light are one and night shines as
when You knit me in my mother's
womb and my very self You knew.

God's knowing is the nightlight where
otherwise white darkness would be.

Home

You are the tree that arches
over the Autumn pond where
graceful geese paddle, their necks
pumping gently before them.

You focus the eye away
from the waddling clumsy geese
who honk like horns into air
that will hold them till hunters

collapse their search for placid
ponds where they would eat, paddle
under trees arched like your arms
still above the placid pond.

Tree Sentencing

    The thrawn trees are gone
          that used to be
the tangle of our privacy.

    Their living roots no longer
          pry beneath
what holds the house

that shivers now
          naked in the variable
April parentheses.

Cut logs and branches
          -- scattered abbreviations –
lie like giant nests fallen

no longer smelling of
          the tawny and dusty
comfort of sparrows

who flutter in circles
          where we cast birdseed
on the metal fire escape.

Next to St. Francis
          on hot steel they dance
looking for a branch –

our street's public trees
          punctuate their blossoming
like exclamation points.

Apocalyptic Deer

Will there be any deer
near town when fear is dark
forest, and walls mark here?

Fear draws tight our towns,
walled smallnesses, mini-
worlds that circle earth, all

space between is a wild-
wood but for occasional
deer who survived our fear.

Bells

    song
           say,
    or bell-ringing

    the way
           they used to

    both hands
           on the rope

    lifting
           whole bodies

    to swinging
           bells

    then down
           touching

    not touching
           the floor

    down and
           up
    singing

Revision

He will be taking the train
from Rome
through the tunnels that lead
to Orte
and on to the light
of Umbria
and Assisi.

He'll live there over thirty years
of summers
in the high house above
the piazza,
Casa Papa Giovanni, where
Don Aldo
will believe he can stay till
there's nothing
to keep coming back for,
no one to know.

And there will be poems
and books of words
and pilgrims will sit
in the garden
at end of day and watch
the sunset
and there will be the scent of
olives, the colors
of window-box flowers
on the balconies,

continued...

young Stefano running after
the bus
till he runs to America,
and Nerina, the lady in blue at
the Bar Minerva, waiting tables
though she's old and tired
holding tight against
the staring lens
and blinding light,
and it will be hot – sweat
running down his back,
the sun a lazar.

And when he returns
the last time, it will be
cold and something
will have changed,
as if weather knew
what he'd become
but for the scratching
of his pen.

Afterword

For me poetry is the shortest word-distance between the writer and the reader. It cuts to the chase and fulfills the admonition of St. Francis in Chapter IX of his Rule: "And let your discourse be brief because the Lord's words were few when he was on earth."

Poetry is succinct. It refracts an essence from within, the way a gemstone does. This essence is, as W.H. Auden says, "a way of happening, a mouth." It is a sacrament of language. Under the appearance of words, of their sounds and ritual meanings, the words of a poem make present another reality hidden inside words themselves. At times it is a reality that cannot be seen or heard, or tasted or touched or smelled; but it can register and be experienced in the soul through the power of imagination acting upon the tropes of poetic tradition, namely: metaphor, analogy, symbol, myth and incantation, or sound.

In other words (literally at times), poetry is news from the soul of the poet to the soul of the listener or reader. It comes from a place other than prose. Often it finds you before you find it. It comes from places archetypal whose images become words. It tells the truth but tells it "slant," as Emily Dickinson says. It sings the words it uses.

continued...

And for Franciscans, their first poet and singer is St. Francis himself. His whole being was that of a poet. He walked and praised as a poet would, singing aloud his spontaneous songs of joy and sorrow. He stored up in his heart the images of earth, water, air, and fire that poured forth toward the end of his life in his "Canticle of the Creatures," the first great Italian poem.

In the same spirit do Franciscan poets make poems and sing them. They try to see the extraordinary in the ordinary, the supernatural in the natural, God in all things. None of which implies a Pollyanna-like or sentimental view of reality that pours holy water over everything trying to cover up the pain or sorrow, the imperfection or evil. On the contrary, poems rise from our real lives, the good and the bad of them, the joy and the sorrow.

This book of poems, then, is a homage not just to the Franciscan way of life in its 800th year, but to life itself as it is lived by one Franciscan in the 21st Century. It celebrates the magic of words to make present on the page what is hidden in the heart, to make visible what is invisible, to sing in good times and bad.

Notes:

Page 9: This poem appeared first in The Cord magazine.

Page 41, epigraph: "Sunt Lachrymae Rerum." There are tears at the heart of things.

Page 51, "Ramage" is a syllabic form of eight lines of roughly ten syllables per line. Certain sounds are repeated throughout the poem. Here it is the assonant sound, "ow."